Organelle

Organelle

Poems by

Donelle Dreese

© 2021 Donelle Dreese. All rights reserved.
This material may not be reproduced in any form, published,
reprinted, recorded, performed, broadcast,
rewritten or redistributed without
the explicit permission of Donelle Dreese.
All such actions are strictly prohibited by law.

Cover design by Shay Culligan

ISBN: 978-1-954353-70-1

Kelsay Books
502 South 1040 East, A-119
American Fork, Utah, 84003
Kelsaybooks.com

Acknowledgments

I am grateful to the following venues in which these poems first appeared, sometimes in different versions:

About Place: "Losing Ground"
Adanna Literary Journal: "Rachel Carson's Love Letters to Dorothy Freeman"
Aldrich Press: "Rachel Carson Kneeling in Sackcloth before the Inquisitors, 1962"
Albatross: "Rachel Carson's White Hyacinth Letter to Dorothy Freeman," "Rachel Carson Responds to Her Critics"
Blue Mountain Review: "Peak Bloom"
The Buddhist Review: "The Body's Silent Conversation with Things," "The Forgetting of Air," "Stories Unknown to Me"
Canary: "The Death of Rachel Carson—April 14, 1964"
Citron Review: "Research Before Google"
Diverse Voices Quarterly: "Almonds," "Survivor"
For a Better World 2018: Poems and Drawings on Peace and Justice: "Love Canal Haiku," "Petra Kelly to Her Green Party Partner and Colleague Gert Bastain," "The Sugared World"
Journal of Kentucky Studies: "The Braun Sisters"
Heritage Acres Memorial Sanctuary Fall 2020 Newsletter: "Don't Wear Black"
Hopper: "Rachel Carson at Woods Hole, Massachusetts, Marine Biological Laboratory, 1929"
Let's Do It Live: Selections from Lexington Poetry Month 2018: "Venus Flytrap"
Lexington Poetry Month: "Biological Concert," "White Cry of Seagulls"
Lime Hawk: "Rachel Carson's Ghost"
Louisville Review: "I've Seen Her Float," "Landslide"
Peacock Journal: "Earth Mothers," "Embryology," "Instead of Crying, She Shovels Mud," "The Patient Universe," "Seasons in the Afterlife"
Potomac Review: "All the Breathless People of the Sun"

Rise Up Review: "The Swallow Experiment, MIT, 1870"
Rogue Agent: "Biophilia"
Runes, A Review of Poetry: "Fox Fire"
Sonora Review: "A World Without Birds"
Split Rock Review: "Maria Carson to Her Daughter, Rachel, Who Attends the Pennsylvania College for Women, 1925," "Organelle"
Thirty Days: The Best of the Tupelo Press 30/30 Project's First Year: "Mind Balloon"
Undead: A Poetry Anthology of Ghouls, Ghosts, and More: "Other Ghosts"

Contents

I. The Carson Poems

Black Folds of the Allegheny	17
Springdale, Pennsylvania	18
Maria Carson to Her Daughter, Rachel, Who Attends the Pennsylvania College for Women, 1925	19
Rachel Carson at Woods Hole, Massachusetts, Marine Biological Laboratory, 1929	20
Biophilia	21
Studying the Life of a Wave	22
Rachel Carson's Love Letters to Dorothy Freeman	23
Almonds	24
All the Breathless People of the Sun	25
Summer in Maine	26
Biological Concert	27
Rachel Carson's White Hyacinth Letter to Dorothy Freeman	28
Instead of Wine	29
A World Without Birds	30
Rachel Carson after Thirteen Hours of Ecstasy with Dorothy Freeman	31
Organelle	32
Losing Ground	33
Field Notes	34
Writing a Book	35
A Million Tentacles Reaching for the Sun	36
Rachel Carson Kneeling in Sackcloth before the Inquisitors, 1962	37
Ceremony for the Planting Moon	38
One Step Closer	39
Rachel Carson Responds to Her Critics	40
Fox Fire	41
White Cry of Seagulls	42
The Death of Rachel Carson—April 14, 1964	43
Resurrection	44

Rachel Carson's Ghost	45
Seasons in the Afterlife	46
Other Ghosts	47

II. The Swallow Experiment

Eleanora's Falcon	51
Space Exploration	52
Research Before Google	53
The Body's Silent Conversation with Things	54
Tracking Signs of Life on the Third Planet from the Sun	55
The Swallow Experiment, MIT, 1870	56
Embryology	57
The Braun Sisters	58
Earth Mothers	59
Love Canal Haiku	60
Growing up in America	61
Survivors	62
Instead of Crying, She Shovels Mud	63
The Forgetting of Air	64
Cosmogenesis: An Abbreviated List	65
Stories Unknown to Me	66
Petra Kelly to Her Green Party Partner and Colleague Gert Bastain	67
Mind Balloon	68
No Trivial Matter	69
I've Seen Her Float	70
The Sugared World	71
Mothering	72
The Venus Flytrap	73
Climate Kids	74
The Ornithologist	76
Instructions for the Winter Solstice	77

Landslide	78
She Is Still Here	79
The Patient Universe	80
Peak Bloom	81
Don't Wear Black	82
About the Author	85

It is good to know that I shall live on even in the minds of many who do not know me, and largely through association with things that are beautiful and lovely.
—Rachel Carson

I.

The Carson Poems

Black Folds of the Allegheny

In summer, milkweed bobbed across the farm
past the gable-roofed barn and chicken coop
chatter, past the orchard of apple and pear,
past my father's vanishing shadow. I followed
it to a path bordered by wilderness crickets
and rabbits that lollipop pink heads of clover.
I followed it until I heard boats murmur,
rocking in low river surf, hidden behind fog
in the black folds of the Allegheny. Sometimes
I walked with my mother who taught me
the musical perchickory of the goldfinch.
I remember her botanizing and bird-watching
while I fingered fossilized shells on riverbanks
and rocky outcroppings of the hillsides. I longed
for a language that would tell me their stories
and name the brave bones behind each
skeletal imprint. Even then, I heard the ocean
calling, reaching out to me at high tide, as if I
were a peculiar clam shell it wanted back.

Springdale, Pennsylvania

Small towns are piano keys slightly out of tune
glowing with the aftertaste of starlight.

They smell of home-grown tomatoes and grass clippings.
They have hoof marks down the center of Main Street.
Their stories are buried in basements in envelopes marked
return to sender. To know their secrets, talk to porch women
who wear white shawl houses around their shoulders.
They know when the babies were born, the year of the drought,
the flood, the unsayable name of the preacher man who killed
his father with a whiskey bottle.

This town is a sleeping cat curled in a river valley.
She only flicks her ears to keep the future away.

Maria Carson to Her Daughter, Rachel, Who Attends the Pennsylvania College for Women, 1925

Go beyond the farm. Go
where words and clover
converge, where books
line walls and knowledge
fountains into the streets.
I'm sorry that your college
clothes are hand-sewn
that we parcel our land
and sell plots to pay tuition
that we've sold the chickens
and the china. I will teach
the children to play piano
for your sake and for theirs
for the world is a crippled
sparrow without its artists.
Your absence has brought
shadow where your words
were mid-day sun. My solace
is that your capacities
will be nourished, that you
will write with a bold
and blossoming pen.
Free yourself of the world
that binds women
and wild creatures within it.

Rachel Carson at Woods Hole, Massachusetts, Marine Biological Laboratory, 1929

It was an ornate church
an altar for moody pools

with corallines, urchins
mollusks and sea fingers.

Every full moon, she watched
the polychaete worms mate

under a dark skin of sea.
Thousands of circles of light

surfaced during this ancient
smoldering night dance.

Holy and terrene affairs
stirred the hub of her being.

She reached out from the soft
cuff of the sea's marbled coat.

She took long shoreline walks
tide-pooling, examining

her own approachable soul
swirling its finger in a tunnel

of deep time, fixing its eyes
on each wave rolling in

nodding its head yes.

Biophilia

Here is a forest in my eye
a gnarled history not seeking
ashes or gardens or sex.

Here is a river in my mouth
with a tree branch for a tonsil
drinking from a fluid pink body.

Here is a thesaurus in my ear
translating words into orchids
germinating, opening, closing.

Here is a moment's fragment
a slice of cloud brought low.
I tap it for rain and turtles fall out.

I live in a house of grass
and this outstretched hair
is all I will give a hard wind.

Studying the Life of a Wave

From a rippled white birth
to a storm roller youth
stone-loaded, hail-shredded
until it calms, reconvenes
into a living, liquid ribbon
ballet dancing over basins
collecting plankton and shark's
teeth, picking up momentum
and stirring shipwreck bones
turning the vessel's peeling pages
into a memoir of the sea floor—
a ghost story with whale song
and the rusted trinkets
of our sunken ancestors
bound for the desert marine.

In its final fathom of life
a tidal knife spreads it thin
freezes it for close analysis
at the feet of a January crone.

Rachel Carson's Love Letters to Dorothy Freeman

Let's call them "apples,"
        those private notes tucked inside
the decorum letters you read to your husband.

Red words and green phrases
        meanings made of mollusk trails
with magic seeds at the core.

I wish the world were less like worm rock
        with its hard honeycomb taffy passageways
deceptive in its appearance as if it were sponge.

Love shouldn't be layered in paper
        behind delicate, aching skin.
It should be Red Delicious, maybe McIntosh.

Almonds

Love came as a Luna moth
a giant silk Saturniidae with a lime smile.

It perched on the painted windowsill
in a milky green suit with almond eyespots.

Its oval avocado wings tapped
and spun the globed porch light

against a leaf and light-studded sky.
With a tiny rip in its wing

it was almost a prince with a broken leg
calling all goddesses for a healing

but it flew away easy as tissue paper
a scatter of small stones in my ear.

Then I remembered your eyes
how I've always loved almonds.

All the Breathless People of the Sun

They sift underneath furniture cushions
passion hunting, gathering lint-caked coins
having fallen from blue jean pockets.

They are sun-lovers who roll in fields
of wild strawberries until their hair turns red
and their eyes are phosphorescent mushrooms.

They are ordinary hermits who swam up
from the bottom of a shivering sea trailing eelgrass
to become all the breathless people of the sun.

They have been sculpted by a cold chisel
that left them eccentric and askew
but brilliant and fearless illuminators.

They are hungry flowers crafting the world.
They drink their water from a cracked cup
and somehow always have enough.

Summer in Maine

Include a wraparound porch
      an infinite field of wild blueberries
arms tanned the color of iced tea
      friendship salad with limed mangoes
drunken lobster on a sandy deck
      ginger to brighten the water supply
storytellers offering alternate endings
      beach walks with God and a labrador
loose locks of dancing sugar kelp
      a pottery shop with lighthouse art
the slick rocks of Penobscot Bay
      white pine and whistles of chickadees
a weathered wooden terrace where two
      lovers left their twilight fingerprints.

Biological Concert

Through winter's monochrome burn
and hibernal holding-in.

Through the spring of flowering magnolia
and voluptuous orchards of summer.

Through October's curtain of copper snow
and fields of frosted pumpkin.

Friendship is the only love.

The rest is a biological concert
pheromone bells tolling in the dark.

Rachel Carson's White Hyacinth Letter to Dorothy Freeman

You know the parable about the man
with only two pennies to his name.

One penny buys the bread
the other, the white hyacinths
because their loveliness is beyond rescue.

You are my white hyacinth.

You are the marginal world
where the moon-drawn tides
spin a million sweet riddles.

Kneeling on a wet carpet of sea moss
I confess the reflected images
in the crystalline pool are of you.

Water rippling with minnow eyes
the spark and waste of the universe
the stone and biology of love.

I need you to know how much I cradle
this flower, how the winter white petals
cool my serious science.

Instead of Wine

Come with me.

Let's drink the landscape
from a honey-lined cup
so hummingbirds wonder
if our lips are flowers.

Let's drink a juice blend
equal parts religion and science
art and economy
human and machine.

Instead of wine, dappled
as it is with the lyric of grapes
let's drink a tall glass
of the world orchestra.

What might a flute taste like?
Cream swirl in blond coffee.

Let's stick a straw into a cloud
and drink the rain before it falls.

Hurry.

A silent spring is coming.

A World Without Birds

They say finch is in the attic running out of songs to sing
tracking circles on sun-dusted floorboards for the good
of all birdkind. Once, bluejay who was jealous of cardinal's
red coat slit his scarlet neck with a honey locust thorn.
Then there was burrowing owl who kept tunneling deep
into earth's mantle until he retired in a magma nest. They
say he was desperate to return to the beginning of creation
and start over. Later, the birds of nautical paradise swooned
for food and died with plastic in their bellies. Have you seen
the tanagers, curlews, and ravens? Where are the plovers,
magpies, and whimbrels? They are all following the whistling
swans through the dark tributaries. In the serene between storms
you can hear them whistle *row, row, row…life is but a dream.*

Rachel Carson after Thirteen Hours of Ecstasy with Dorothy Freeman

I built a fortress around those thirteen hours
as if the minutes were sewn with magic yarn.

Afterward, I slept a motionless flame
dreaming of giving her a seaweed bracelet

braided in the intertidal zone where periwinkle
snails graze on algae and barnacle larvae.

She is the anchor for a ship driven to capsize
rare as an undamaged angel wing, a shell

home to a clam that burrows deep into clay
and glows green from its shoreline hideaway.

Of all the wonders that occupy the sea's edge
she is the most exquisite air-breather.

Organelle

This is about fish that glow in the dark
how the phosphorescent plankton
in their bellies transforms them into a school
of tiny souls spinning around seaweed
in an ocean wave shaped like a question mark
while science turns its clinical head away
looks to the ringed moon for answers
fingers to its neck, searching for gills.

This is about getting to know each other
again as a planetary imperative
a cell membrane circling a globe
worlds within worlds, organs within organs
mitochondria coughing up smoke
seagulls swooping the surf
roses falling, still dripping of love.

This is about the smallest cell traveling
around the world and seeing itself
in a lemon tree, dirt, or a pack of wolves
as earth hatches clouds, country roads
and its organelle, from the salted mountain
to the dog barking at a strawberry moon
both familiar and phenomenal.

Losing Ground

While we are seaside, quiet outside looking in
we can save ourselves before our bones bleach

before our coral architecture grays. We can pray
for our skeletons to bathe in clean tropical blood

transform denial into blue-green moss
fragrant as a florist, smart as a forest exhale.

The man with the gold-plated pen in his hand
is a behind-the-scenes laughing back row crow

poking the sandbag barriers surrounding islands
standing near the coffin thinking it will confess.

Science is not a battleground for businessmen
nor a sanctuary for a simmering stew of beliefs.

Watch, as the tired street pumps in Miami
send drums of marine water back out to sea.

Field Notes

Hillsides ushering rain
into a pulsing watershed.

Free beaches, crashing surf.
Yellow pollen catching fire.

Nectarine sprays in deep afternoon.
Heron shadows on a riverbank.

Rocky creeks to cross on foot.
A blush of summer tomatoes.

Crescendos of October withering.
Stone holy paths, crags of understory.

Evergreen needles piercing
the mind's heavy snow loft.

Circles of people, not rows.
Art, that merciful minister.

Whispers so luminous, blades of grass
listen beneath a coverlet of snow.

Love, that drop in the bucket
soothing a starving sea.

Writing a Book

There may be a fracture inside
salt-laced and sea-carved.

There may be estranged houses
wordless rooms to avoid.

After hours of pulverizing shells
there may only be a few grains of sand.

Bring aloes and silver for mornings of burn.
Fan the lesser fires with woven seagrass.

In the evening, return to lyric forests.
Draft a path through the underbrush.

Relish that you have time to hunt
wild mushrooms you can eat

that you know the difference
between poison and pleasure

even when only a few morels
deliver eloquent spores.

A Million Tentacles Reaching for the Sun

Sea coral inhabits compact colonies
dressed in algae for the world's most
courageous color display. The polyps
cloned by the thousands are articulate
reef-builders, host to feather and basket
stars that capture plankton and bloom
a million tentacles reaching for the sun.
In the distance, the brain coral utters
a pale thought, but still brighter than
we are, as seagulls stir white tornadoes
over the sand, holler sirens into the air.

Rachel Carson Kneeling in Sackcloth before the Inquisitors, 1962

The report from the flesh is in
my breast, my body toxic

a DDT groundwater plume
and stinking baptism

in a lagoon that smells
like an old shoe.

You ask me about my research
accuse me of housing the feral

jam jars full of crickets
in spinster cupboards

my endocrine outbursts
in need of rest.

Did you expect me to sleep
on a bed of unhammered nails?

You go home to strawberry shortcake
cookie jars, eat fish from rivers

beneath gooseneck smokestacks
call me hysterical.

Ceremony for the Planting Moon

Fall to the ground. Dig a dream hole. Plant yourself feet first.
Become a bead of seed in buoyant loam, a willowed sculpture
or faceless forest mystic. Cup your own biome in your hands,
hold it close to your chest. Let pieces of earth cling to your belly,
impress you with mineral crumbles. Close your eyes and conjure
a whole world riding on the silver spine of a minnow. Imagine
seaweed the same color as your hair. Caress the cool locks
over your heart's hot edges. Remember yourself as botanical,
as chrysalis, as alchemist. Envision the walnut woods
and thistled dawn where you were born.

Then, grow hardwood brave.

One Step Closer

We are looking at a thousand geese resting on water.
Some are hunting silvery fleeting fishes. Some have storied
plant riddles smudged on their paddled feet. Some are cradling
moss, goslings, and remote bits of earth in the flightless folds
of their feathers. There's so much to live for. As long as a candle
burns, the swing of its flame is speaking. The utterance will
be heard by those who are brave, by those who have taken
a song's finest lyrics and learned to sing them without collapsing,
by those who grieve for the lost arm of a starfish. Every day
we move one step closer to what's possible—wind, wood, water,
the knowledge of clay. The shape of things is out of our hands,
but here we sit with the potter to see if our skin has softened
on the spinning wheel.

Rachel Carson Responds to Her Critics

Gentleman, I've spotted you in my gaslight
held the burning match for too long.

Pity, that you deem it a heresy to care
more about birds than business.

But I do remember that you too
were once a pure blue egg

warm and opening beneath a belly of fur.
I understand that you too

were once a desperate cry from the crib
when your mother was numb and spent.

Still, I've wondered how many miles from mercy
is the buried beggar inside of you

who can be touched by kindness
on a cold highway.

When you stand before me I see
an allergy even the drenched earth can't cure.

My mouth, sour with bad medicine
sweetens when I say, *no more.*

Fox Fire

Resentment is a briar
a peppery brine
a bitter and thorny lock-jaw
whose words cross like lattice-work
and leave you running
to cotton fields for breathing space.

It is a hollow vestibule
dressed in a spiny frostbelt

a graverobber making meals
from crushed bones

a sea rover pacing the deck
of a crepe paper sail.

I'm going to turn it into fox fire
a languid composite mesh
born from its sultry rot
giving off just enough glint
to map the way out.

White Cry of Seagulls

Seashells—miniature temples I crawl into to pray.

Once I pulled a Florida Cone from a cat's mouth
thinking she was hungry for crab meat.

Then, there was the day I thought I lost you
between the boardwalk and breakers.

You almost kissed me in a field of tidal mist
before the gulls came nipping in the night.

Today's prayer holds iridescence of abalone.
Your luster still haunts me when it rains.

I dust each shell with fingertips, peek inside
the hollow, remember the white cry of seagulls.

Clean and unfractured, memories pearl.
I remember the sun, but not the burn.

The Death of Rachel Carson—April 14, 1964

The battle of living things against cancer began so
long ago that its origin is lost in time.
—Rachel Carson

It had spread to her liver.
She never read the last letter

from Dorothy, the one that said—
I have come to a great sense of peace about you.

She said *for all at last return to the sea.*
Then death came whale-bursting

into her life, metastasizing
stirring its cellular gravel.

Denial is a disorderly thief
and resistance turns water to lead

so she let the thing flow through her
plunged her tired arm into the mud

felt the cool, thick mercy
against her skin, waited for the clay pack

to reclaim her fingerprints
until pain became impossible.

Resurrection

Layers of skin fell from the corners
of her mouth, became tangled in her hair
as warm snowflakes. When she stood,
luminous skin peeled to the floor in papery
layers around her feet as beech bark
or coconut. She rose to examine herself.

The afterlife is awash with intelligent fish
dazed after being caught in a line. Her body
for an instant became sage and white fire.

What will I do with my auspicious life now?

Rachel Carson's Ghost

She crossed the Allegheny River
wearing anklets of river grass.

I followed her through Springdale
on a trail of broken crab claws

bits of sea glass and bones of fishes.
She paused at a fracking field

where the aquifer detonation
rocked a chemical earthquake

turned her white glow to gray.
She faded then, the way a ribbon

of mist wilts over evergreen,
but the look in her eye was a cold ring

an alarm without an answer
a scream without a mouth.

Seasons in the Afterlife

A trail of dewed apples
      leads to a honeycomb
      that slow drips golden eggs
      onto dandelion greens.

Roses roll down rooftops
      from a floral rain. Fragrance
      spreads like sea foam and fog
      across jade throats of grass.

A violin bow in November stirs
      leaves into singing whirlpools
      and punctures the heart
      of a yellow mum.

The great hush of winter
      sits in a vast snowfield
      under the limb of an evergreen
      waits for the black call of crows.

Other Ghosts

You and me and the other ghosts
make backyard trees puff and shush

a blackberry ocean of roaring woods
where hazel-winged birds

gather for a branch dance on limbs
of oak and walnut chocolate spoons.

When they flock away as one
feathered blanket lifting

the understory rises and sighs
while you and me and the other ghosts

inhale the musky woodland swell
hum grassy songs and sway.

II.

The Swallow Experiment

Eleanora's Falcon

for Eleanor of Arborea

At any given moment, a bird is singing.
The song is a firework piping under a green canopy.
A scream hurled out to sea, a trumpet for morning sun.
The singer could be a magpie, an avocet, a blackbird, a loon.
It whistles whether the field mouse stops to listen or not.
It cries for the holy tug toward creation.
It yodels without us, yet we still feel the warble in our throats.
It trills into the mossy tree hollow, under the acoustic cliff.
It coos in a bed of twig, cotton, and brunette hair.
It chirrups without wanting to change the world.
It doesn't carol for the record, for the catalog, for us.
It whip-poor-wills a sandy-tongued ballad, unravelling with pitch.
It's Eleanora's Falcon scrawling a calligraphy of shrieks
across a blue valley of sky.

Space Exploration

for Henrietta Swan Leavitt

Once, while measuring the luminosity of stars
I discovered a collection of daydreams housed
in a library suspended within the Milky Way's
glistening necklace. Visible, but unwearable.
Like any astronomer, I have questions about who
I am and who you are. My scholarly midnights
are spent researching the visual and aural acuity
of owls to learn clarity. If I could grow plumage
with the same feather structure, I could fly beyond
the closest star and touch the veil with an open
claw. Maybe then, I might know you. I might
know me. I could return to the realm of bark
and grass as the sun creeps down into its basin
below the fingernails of trees. Answer me this—
have I spent too much time in the sky?

Research Before Google

A library is a repository of medicine for the mind
—Greek Proverb

Metal shelves shoulder to shoulder
measured for browsing space

in rows fill a broad room
with the scent of book binding

and history. One isle contains
a footstool, a note pad, and a girl.

The privacy choreographed
but not absolute. She takes it

all in, a marathon runner
with each book a roadside vista

on a scenic highway where she
must stop for a blessing.

The boy in the next aisle
closes his eyes, inhales

her perfume, simple and clean
citrus and spring rain.

He traces an isolated doodle
waits like a frozen river.

The Body's Silent Conversation with Things

Today, I traced your image
in the morning air
birthing your summer
form in front of me
with frightened hands. I hope
for a moment, wherever
you were, you felt your body
being whispered
by the breathable things
that surround you,
that you stopped your work
when you felt my palm
press tree saplings
into the habitat
of your heart. Someday,
I might say it out loud. I might
lay the language down
in front of you as a timbered
path carpeted in moss,
but today, I rely
on the body's silent conversation
with things, the tilt toward
the outer edges
of the known world,
the lean into love's broadleaf
fingerprint, all the while
my oak and maple hips
sway in concert with wild
grasses as I walk.

Tracking Signs of Life on the Third Planet from the Sun

A road, a line of weeds up the center,
the withered words of concrete.

Two fawns feeding on ground cover
flicking their ears at honeybee buzz.

A gray cat with four white paws
dipped in a pool of marigolds.

A silent seagull shifting on a wire,
waits for water, wants for home.

Mailboxes, floral-framed or bare-boned,
mouths open, asking for handouts.

A graveyard of rolling grass and speckled stone,
a shadow in the peripheral eye, a ghost.

Old men, seated statues in parked trucks,
dead-pan faces forward, already gone.

The Swallow Experiment, MIT, 1870

for Ellen Swallow Richards

They said she was vapor, not form,
a *special student,* a tuition-free experiment.

She swept floors in bearded halls
mended her professor's trousers
sewed the thick buttons back on
in between chemistry equations.

She studied in a laboratory labeled
for women, taught classes for free
purified water among molecules
of high brows and low expectations.

I search for her name in a drinking glass
looking for the emergence story
spinning around speck and iota.

Matriculation must have seemed
impossible, a wet candle wick.

And yet experiments are like that—
open-faced flames burning through
the fat wax of foregone conclusions.

Embryology

You step into a birdhouse
second womb
acorn cup of warm blood
a nest to rest
before time disfigures
your sage and aging embryo.
You find a sea
of seeds and twigs
dirt memories to kick with the foot
a suspended
boughless universe for warbling
one hypothesis at a time.
You are an idea
cradled in a wooden envelope.
A potential. A budding.
Then, the flutter
in your rusted underwing drums
stirs a chestnut feather cloud
as the house shakes
squeezes, launches
your clumsy ambitionist
out the door.
There must be a better way
to learn how to fly.

The Braun Sisters

for Annette and Lucy Braun

What would Lucy say about floristics
now that the old growth forests are fleeing

taking their soft bones and medicines with them?
I see the headstones at Spring Grove Cemetery

above the pulp and rhizome of Lucy and Annette.
I think of Lucy's fight for Kentucky's deciduous

think of her sister, Annette, who told the stories
of moths, how their wings are scaled, not dusted

how their pale-dressed patterns have no desire
to dance for the sun, but somewhere in Ohio

or Kentucky, they still walk the forests reciting
the names and properties of every living thing.

Red Cedar, Bee Balm, Cinnamon Fern.
Lucy is collecting herbarium specimens

while Annette is reading Lucy's essays
to see if moths fly out of them.

Earth Mothers

They came in early spring.
They asked the hard, dry fields
to be patient. They folded dirt
into buckets and planted seeds
not knowing if the green shoots
of prayer would bear fruit. They
surrounded a tree swallow's cradle
packed with eggs and sang songs
in low-throated melodies of birth.
They brought with them tones
of the sea hoping the memories
of marshlands would feed
the waterfowl. The earth mothers
come every spring and we don't
see them, rowing and sowing,
dangling spit on their fields
when the rain doesn't come.
They are fathers too, with boot
prints that circle the barn, eyes
reminiscent of hunger pangs
beneath a naked rib cage,
eyes like dark fire.

Love Canal Haiku

for Lois Gibbs

Bricklayer's daughter
boat-rocker from Love Canal
blue collar shy

Land for a dollar
sold to a school for children
chemical graveyard

Years of hard rain
ooze and rusted drums surfaced
playground sickness

Knuckles knocked on doors
self-taught environmentalists
mobilized mothers

Picketing power
civil disobedience
asbestos jail cell

Here's a child's coffin
for the Governor's office
wooden petition

Grassroots warrior
the mother of superfund
history maker

Growing up in America

On a bed of grass, she watches hope float away
in the basket of a hot air balloon. She imagines
it landing in the middle of the ocean where
it suffocates in folds, filling with water, swaying
on the way down. She wonders if she should follow
it, but chooses to contemplate winter, how loss
positions itself on snow so she can see it clearly
and measure the depths of its icy impressions.
The distance between her white divided house
and the summer grass will take decades to cross.
She may never return, choosing to roam redwoods
with fox and doe, palming apple and plum to snuff
all hungers, done with crayons and candy. The streets
far away are popping with scarlet and the schools
are peppered with puncture wounds. Each day
is a garden of beautiful and terrible things.

Survivors

Some days are raw hot wind
dark maroon blossoms of moods

bordering on mechanical
and here we are blinking

trying to free gummed lashes
from something flying in the air

a sour mash of fear and fatigue.
I know you had to walk through

a labyrinth of knives, but look
your ankles are still smooth.

You are still warm and awake
after listening to the ocean moan

after treading the web lines of a leaf
and wearing a stinging fur of snow.

The lanterns are underwater
but they illuminate the starfish

suspended near the surface
so we can see what we are given.

The virtuosity of another day
to make it right this time.

Instead of Crying, She Shovels Mud

for Sangduen "Lek" Chailert

Elephants rumble
in flat grass fields.

Skin—earthy, ancient
slick with fog
grasshopper rain.

Instead of crying
she shovels mud
builds sanctuaries
homes for herds
and snout-swinging
curious calves
lingering near pools
of purple fruit
and shaman dust.

Ghost men watch
from poaching posts
eyeing the ivory.

Her touch is a balm
against the onslaught.

If only she could
sleep standing up.

The Forgetting of Air

I am inside a tight fold of green leaves wanting to open.
I am a body of floating embryos that move from limb
to limb, heart to mouth, rain-bathing like mourning doves.
My dreams are filled with barriers crumbling, canyons
closing, the sensation of six feet dissolving to zero.
My days are filled with the forgetting of air, forgetting
to breathe, forgetting an old life. Even in summer,
there is a slight chill. I drink mangoes, orchids, colors
that are in season. This is what I want to know—if I drink
the blue of an angry jay, will I become hostile? A lifetime
can live in six feet of air. Each time the air comes back
to me, I remember that someone once left a box of ripe
peaches on my doorstep. I can still smell the nectar.
The inhale keeps me alive.

Cosmogenesis: An Abbreviated List

Velvet planet floating.

Sun, swinging in solar orbit.

Insects in dirt orchestra.

Bowing of serpentine rivers.

Milky Way, a string of chandeliered palace rooms.

Time, war, time, war.

Brail vocabulary of tree bark.

Seasonal expression, or, the liturgy of plants.

Blooming of the lilies.

Crop circles and other disrupters.

Oceans lifting their skirts.

Fiery grasslands and tornadic dust.

Power and plunder, or, consciousness collapse.

Pollution, a settled village.

Children activists in streets.

Mountains on trial for moving.

Extinction.

Ours.

Stories Unknown to Me

I'm thinking about the stories I will never hear:

The floral origins of your birth, the verdant colors and precocious
cries of your childhood, the moment your faith jangled clear
in your mind like a sanctified tambourine or rain dancing inside
the blushing body of a cloud. I won't hear about your lakes
of loves, the shallow and placid, nor the long and legendary.
I won't hear about how you became a virtuoso, a conductor
of resonant, symphonious souls, nor the tale of the immortal
mistake that became your impossible lotus flower, or the regret
that sits in the bottom of your heart as a haunted shipwreck,
now home to hard and soft coral. I won't hear how you became
death's graceful ally, or how you raised a calf who became a sturdy
elk with velvet on his antlers.

I will never know many stories, except this one. One day,
for a moment, you looked at me and wondered, who is she?

Petra Kelly to Her Green Party Partner and Colleague Gert Bastain

I want to end this questioning
of you killing me.

You, with your rose and bone fingers
smoke-smudged, old fruit.

It is always the lover
with gunpowder on his hands.

Had living in my shadow grown
dim, so quiet and opaque?

They called me Jeanne d' Arc
an endangered person

so the murder could have been staged.
It could have been the authors

of the death threat letters who fume
with contempt for the Green party.

The Dalai Lama said to me
Keep going. I'll meditate for you.

I wrote a book to infuse
spirit into the body politic.

But who left the typewriter humming?
Who pressed the trigger and final key?

Was it you, my partner, my life, my love?
Was it your hand that encircled the gun as if curled for a glass of wine?

Mind Balloon

I'm no shrinking violet!
        Overheard in a hallway
                that was not a garden.

Good to know, but are you the corpse flower
        largest of all flowers, rare as ghost orchids
                but smells of rotting flesh

        are you consciousness expanding
                a well-kneaded intellectual bread batter
                      slowly bubbling and browning over
                the side of the baking dish

        or a mind balloon over-puffed and wind-inflated
                with hot gusts, its translucent thin skin
                      showing psyche stretch marks?

I wonder if you are sorry
        for the aggressive crop-dusting
                if you've ever tried decaf?

        I have a safety pin in my pocket.
I'm not the only one.

No Trivial Matter

Mount Kenya is a shy mountain
hidden behind clouds
the source of Kenya's rivers
a holy land for the Kikuyus
who believe God dwells
on the mountain and everything
good flows from it.

When the missionaries came
they said, "God dwells in heaven."

They have been looking for heaven
but have not found it.

During the long, dark decades
it was believed the religious systems
were sinful, barbaric, savage.

But without a culture, one is a slave
one who has collaborated with the slave trader
disinherited, with nothing to pass on.

This is no trivial matter
reviving pottery and dancing
reclaiming an essence
not seen through the mirror
of missionaries.

A found poem from Wangari Maathai's essay "The Cracked Mirror,"
Resurgence Magazine*, November 11, 2004.*

I've Seen Her Float

Then one day she became breakable
as a sparrow's breastbone.

I saw her throw love at a mirror
hoping it would stick, but it snailed south

where a flock of apologies cycloned
around her waist like a tape measure.

She is silk hope falling onto slick clay
a sailboat waiting for the mast to unfold.

She will find buoyancy, I know it.
I've seen her float.
.

The Sugared World

for Phyllis Mullenix

What happens when research is so bright
it turns toothpaste into white soot?

It should have blackened the industry
behind the smile of unsound science.

It should have saved betrayed mothers
who poured poison water into baby
cups thinking it would postpone the rot
and decay of the sugared world.

It should have saved the workers
at Hurricane Creek, Virginia who waded
in the liquid lie of the factory before
it shattered and shivered their nerves.

But a scientist was fired, unfunded
accused of hysterics from long hours
spent charting the convulsions of rats.

Her work was squeezed, brushed, spit
out to preserve the toxic experiments
of Harold Hodge—the father of fluoride
whose chemical research informed
the making of the atomic bomb.

The myth swims in the water supply
where it stays a savior for the sweet tooth
a barbed shrub behind a wall of honeysuckle

holy water still used for blessings
upon entering the church and leaving.

Mothering

The tomatoes are bold garnet globes.
Last year they were weathered eggs

not sure if they wanted to hatch.
The cucumbers drip behind sun-singed

leaves that spill over a trellis. Despite
the ragged cloak, they soldier on—

a strong army. Next year, the blueberry
bushes may deliver only purple stones.

The peppers may need mothering.
The herbs may fuss in their beds.

I think of what needs tending. It's never
the same year to year. How is my heart?

The house? Is a bat burrowing in the attic?
Is a clean cry stuck in the dry pocket

of my throat? The zucchini wants me
to pollinate, so I mate the gold blossoms.

I watch what is nesting in my life
which bird needs a push to fly.

The Venus Flytrap

She thinks I will get lost in her bog.
I gather peat moss and leave.
A muddy encounter.

She wants me to visit her garden.
I wave from the highway.
A technical move.

She hopes I will walk into her rage.
I am the trigger, not the meal.
A cricket's adieu.

She tells me she wants stillness.
She is waiting for meat.
A carnivorous heart.

Climate Kids

for Greta Thunberg

We might become the butterflies
that couldn't scatter fast enough
from the decadent milkweed
that leaned over the train tracks.

Floss and wings shattered by steel.

At least for now, earthworms
are still creating new soil by eating
their way through leaf litter.

Dragonflies still give nimble
pond performances.

Barn swallows still gather mud
on their tongues to build homes
in the underbellies of broken bridges.

But we live on the edge
of a snowflake poised to melt
counting dangers as a band
of barnacles stuck to a cracked hull.

We have studied the science
and decided we want to live
while you spread peanut butter
as if you are slowly going blind.

Do something.

This is not a fixed moon.
Your own emerald heart is on fire.

See the dimming fireflies.
See we are beautiful.

See we are dying.

The Ornithologist

Today might include a walk in the woods
the forest, a paragon of symmetry, artistry
bird mimicry and footwork of deer.

It might include a stab of memory
daggers thrown at me, front and back
now a pile of pale stones and bones.

Memory is merely a musing
an idea that passes like clouds
when the past has no stone to throw.

My brain is pulsing with orchid blood
words looted from lyrics, neuron hum
a perceived problem I hope to unpuzzle.

The future is also just thinking
an idea that passes like clouds
the come and go of noise and hush.

Presence may not be philosophical
but rather zoological, an ornithologist
discovering a new species of bird.

Instructions for the Winter Solstice

Right now, ask an evergreen
if it wants to live forever
listen to the answer.

Look into the heart of an apple
see the whole orchard
sip its cider on the dark solstice.

Notice your fingerprint
how your personal swirls
resemble time rings on a tree.

Walk fog-banked streets
let clouds hang from your
shattered, outstretched arms.

Cup the gray into your body
become weightless, gothic
a dolphin swimming in silver.

Remember you are an eclipse
yes, sterling as that.

Landslide

with thanks to Stevie Nicks

I am getting older too
but not so old that my dreams
can't swing on a hammock

tied between two trees
one harmony, one melody
and get lyric-lost in a song

about hills, years, and reflecting
snow, not so old that I'm waiting
for the landslide of topsoil

collagen-drained and cliff-hanging
to sag until my stones appear
making my mountains unrecognizable

not so old that I'm afraid of change
afraid of losing you after
so much snowfall, heavy

as the drifts are getting, still
anchored by roots planted
in the season of sure things.

She Is Still Here

for Mary Oliver

She never sought the spotlight.
It followed her, dropping mangoes
in her lap that she would use

in a poem, rather than eat.
It was bliss to walk the fog bank
of Blackwater Pond in morning

follow fox through braided sticks
track verses on barnacled beaches
distill all hope and wisdom

from the flight of a hummingbird.
Family was a flock of geese.
Molly for forty years.

Percy returning home with
a grizzled skull in his mouth.
Deer, so close she felt the puff

of their breath on her fingers.
She is still here reading tree bark
shagbarks and walnuts

singing into swollen rivers
reaching into stone pockets
pulling out starfish and stories

reminding us at every turn
to pay attention, this is our
endless and proper work.

The Patient Universe

for Jane Goodall

Knowledge in Tanzania
was an envelope sealed with wax.

She held the flame close enough
long enough, without burning it

until her light unfolded the forest canopy
unzipped the greens gowns of Gombe.

After a year, gorillas went to her for bananas
taught her their language, groomed her

while the patient universe grew its hair
and stretched again its long, starry legs.

Peak Bloom

The house backs into the woods.

We bring our soft spirits and iced teas
try to imagine what it was like before
this singing cicada wall of green.

Only a few months ago
it was all naked twig and trunk
knuckled bark, brown and gray.

We watch a spotted fawn
bed down in a field of purple
coneflower, waiting for mother.

Yesterday, we saw a coyote stalk
through clover where goldfinches
bob and butterflies braid.

We sit without speaking
witness the rage between
bird and squirrel echo on.

Remember when we had our own
small fires that we tried to extinguish
with flowers and retreats into trees?

Now we sit quiet and listen
watch the peak bloom wither.

Don't Wear Black

I am preparing the fireflies for a final blink
the wolf, a final trot on a prairie, a final heron
perch at the skirt of a pond backlit by moonrise.
Soon, I will become my composer, wear tree
roots as bracelets, be tugged into an arboretum
to eternize as woodland pulp. Isn't it extraordinary?
By then, death will have broken open and bled
its rainstorm, lost its slow apology. Heart and mouth.
The mound shaping my decay might be an overlay
of yarrow, ochre leaf ash from yesterday's autumn
dirt tracked by a flock of starlings. Groundwork.
Perhaps I will be compost of rose petal and bird.
Even you, my friend, whose microbial cocktails
and textures mix with mine. Let's meet in the woods
in the afterlife. We can smile from the other side
of the veil, wonder why we ever thought we were
small. Who knows why the luna moth has only one
week to live. For now, I stand my ground. But someday
the grape of summer will go to raisin, string its vine
in the substratum. Please. No casket. No embalming.
No concrete vault to stop my arms from slowly
threading clay. And please. Don't wear black.
Bring your color. All of it. Let every green grave
be a grand piano with moss on its keys. After
a long life, you might hear songs, long to play.

About the Author

Donelle Dreese is a poet, novelist, essayist, and Professor of English at Northern Kentucky University where she teaches multicultural and inclusive literatures, environmental literature, ecocriticism, American women poets, and literature & film. She is the author of several poetry collections, including *Sophrosyne* (Aldrich 2015). Her creative work has appeared in a wide variety of literary journals including *Potomac Review, Roanoke Review, Louisville Review,* and *Quiddity International.* In her free time, Donelle serves as Vice President of Heritage Acres Memorial Sanctuary, Cincinnati's only dedicated natural burial preserve.

www.ingramcontent.com/pod-product-compliance
Lightning Source LLC
Chambersburg PA
CBHW032010080426
42735CB00007B/562